EXPLORING THE WOODS

CHILDREN'S SCIENCE & NATURE

BABY PROFESSOR

EDUCATION KIDS

Speedy Publishing LLC

40 E. Main St. #1156

Newark, DE 19711

www.speedypublishing.com

Copyright 2016

THE AMAZING WOODS

What is a forest?
How does it differ from a row of trees, or an apple orchard, or one tree planted in a pot?

Kids, let's visit the wilderness. It has so much to offer. The wild beauty of nature can capture the heart of those who move through it.

READ ON AND EXPLORE THE WOODS.

Have you experienced walking through the woods? It conveys magic.

The atmosphere is a bit dark. The quietness makes you feel your solitary moments. Its grandeur is captivating.

In almost every continent in the world, you can find forests. The amazing splendor of the woods serves as the habitats for other plants, for insects, and for animals large and small.

The woods are also areas in the wild just like forests. However, we use "woods" to describe a smaller area than what a forest covers. An even smaller area of trees might be called a "grove", a "plantation", or a "copse".

Woodland normally has a wide ranges of trees, some growing close together. These trees clean the air we breathe.

Shrubs, grasses and underbrush also flourish in these amazing areas of the Earth. It is part of nature's bounty.

The woods, like the forests, are a home to many kinds of animals, plants, insects, and birds.

The woods can be made up mainly of deciduous trees, which lose their leaves in the winter, or evergreens.

Forests and woods are parts of nature that helps the whole Earth survive. This is pretty magnificent. Both areas carry nature.

The woods can be a perfect place for walking and exploration. It is invigorating to take a walk in the woods with your family. It is worth the experience and adventure.

In doing this, try to leave no trace that you have been there. Stop and listen to the wind, the birds, the sound of running water. Let the woods speak to you.

Here are some things you might love doing in the woods with your family.

PICNIC

Spread out a blanket under a tree and take your lunch or snacks. Or you may share food together under the warm sun. However, only light a fire in a fire pit or other safe area: you don't want to cause a forest fire!

CLEAN THE WOODS

You can do this earth-friendly act with your family. Collecting trash in the woods is a means of helping Mother Earth. It makes you a good steward. Bring trash bags and gloves to do your part to help the woods look nice.

TAKE PHOTOS

As you interact with the natural environment, you can take turns taking pictures of nature. A digital camera or the camera on your phone will record the beauty of the woods.

BIRD WATCHING

Bring binoculars with you. Focus your gadgets to the amazing colorful birds and witness their graceful flight among the trees. Listen for their songs. This is totally a fantastic experience.

Exploring the woods will make you realize how impressive nature really is. The living trees bring total outdoor satisfaction. Plan your visit now.

Made in the USA
Monee, IL
22 June 2021